GRITS

Philip Tanner

Illustrations by Cindy Nielsen

Dedication

I want to dedicate this book to my wonderful wife and beautiful daughter. Thank you for your love and support through COVID-19 and my deployment in 2020.

Have you ever eaten grits?

I eat grits for breakfast,
lunch, and
dinner time.

Grits are sticky,
they get everywhere!

Sometimes grits end up getting all over my bear.

I try to spoon the grits to my mouth. They slip off and take a trip, heading down south.

Sometimes the grits go up my nose.
Then they end up between my toes.

Grits get stuck in my
eyelashes.

I think they make stylish
mustaches.

I try to eat grits all prim
and proper.

Mommy is quickly becoming an expert mopper.

When my parents are not watching, I put the grits on my head.

Mommy makes me bathe so they do not end up in my bed.

Grits are so sticky!
They get everywhere.
They even stick to my
derriere!

THE END

If you enjoyed this book, please
leave a review on Amazon.

About the Author

Philip Tanner is a husband to a wonderful woman and father to a beautiful girl. He graduated from Newberry College with a BA in History, earned his MS in Criminal Justice from Charleston Southern University while attending The Citadel's ROTC program where he earned his commission. Throughout his lifetime, he has worked on farms, volunteered as a firefighter, flown helicopters, but his biggest adventure of all, is being a father.

About the Illustrator

My passion and experiences for art include a wide array of mediums. One of my new all time favorites is drawing illustrations for Children's Books. This is fueled by my love of God, Family and People, especially my granddaughter, Thea. My hope is to engage the viewer into an enjoyable experience, appreciating God's creations.

The Elusive Gecko

Philip Tanner
Illustrated by Cindy Nielsen

Scan QR Code
to purchase on
amazon.com

Made in United States
Orlando, FL
22 March 2026